CHRISTMAS En

Contemporary Arrangements of Christmas Favorites

BOOK 1

arranged by
Melody Bober

CONTENTS

Silent Night

Music by
Franz Grüber

3

FF1197

4

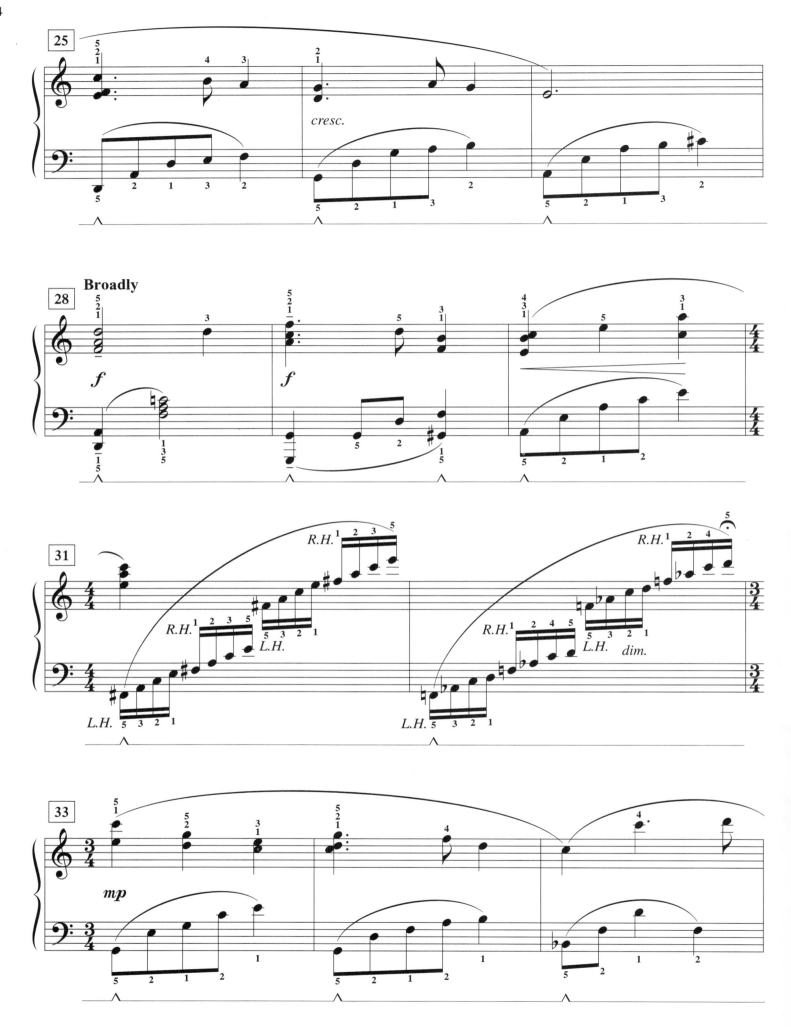

O Come, All Ye Faithful
Adeste Fideles

Wade's *Cantus Diversi*
Transcribed by
F. Oakeley

7

FF1197

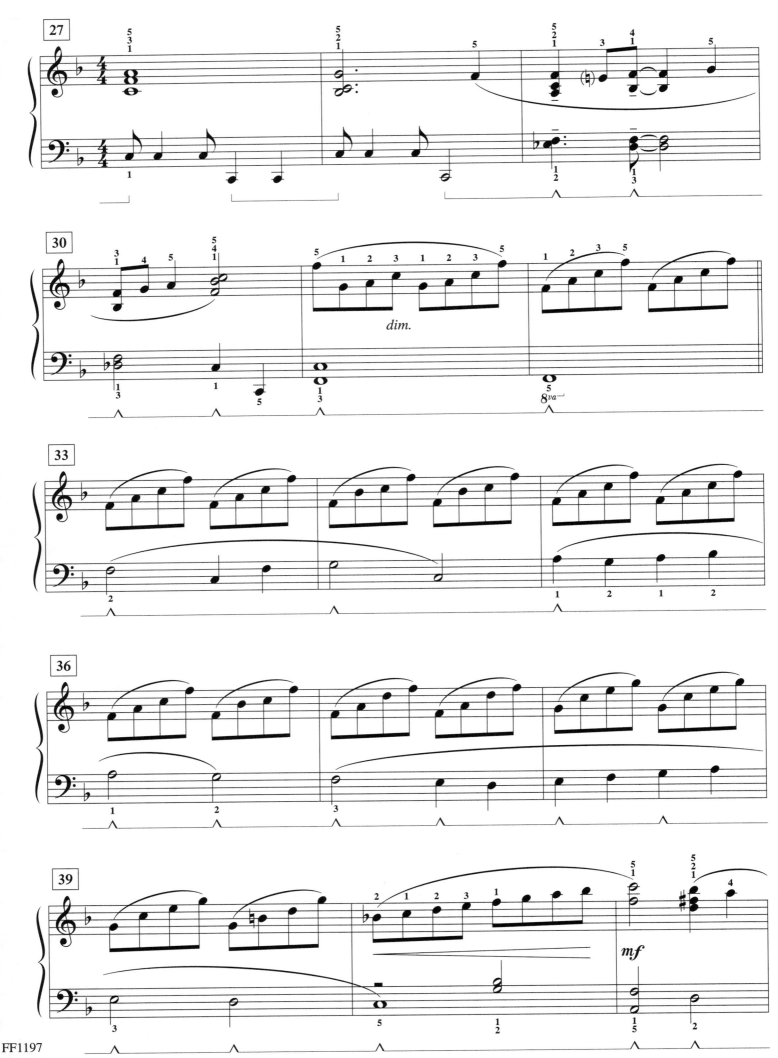

We Three Kings of Orient Are

Words and Music by
J. H. Hopkins, Jr.

12

Hark! The Herald Angels Sing

Felix Mendelssohn
and
Chas. Wesley

16

FF1197

17

FF1197

O Little Town of Bethlehem

L. H. Redner

Angels We Have Heard on High

Traditional French

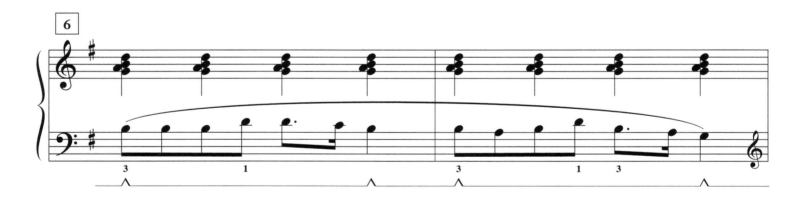

24

FF1197

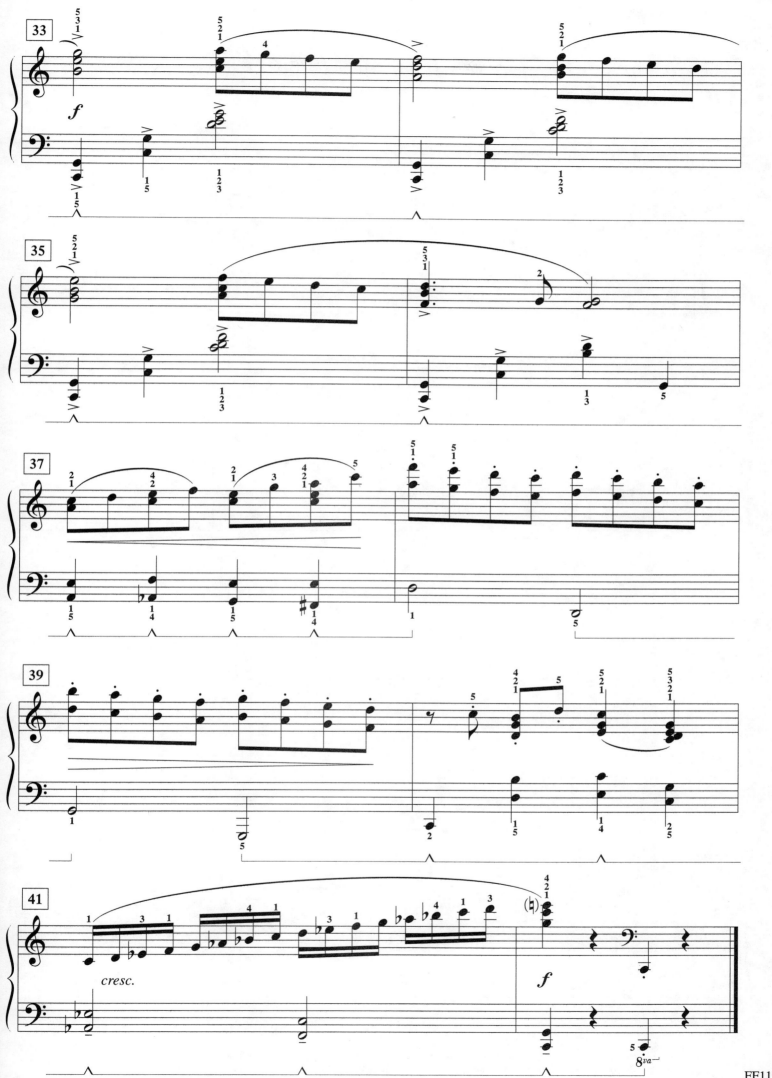

25

FF1197

Go Tell It on the Mountain

Traditional

28

FF1197

29

FF1197

Sing Noël, Noël

Traditional French

32

HEAVEN ON EARTH

Words and Music by
MELISSA ETHERIDGE

WE ARE THE ONES

Words and Music by
MELISSA ETHERIDGE

82

ONLY LOVE

Words and Music by
MELISSA ETHERIDGE

TO BE LOVED

Words and Music by
MELISSA ETHERIDGE

Moderately fast

Wel-come to the plan - et earth, __ wel-come to the he - ro's fall, __

GENTLY WE ROW

Words and Music by
MELISSA ETHERIDGE

99